What Do You Want to Be
When You Grow Up?

This one is for Ashima Narain, and the three little Spacies.—Jerry Pinto

To Vinod Rajagopalan and his dreams.—Ashok Rajagopalan

TALKING CUB
Published by Speaking Tiger Books LLP
125A, Ground Floor, Shahpur Jat
New Delhi 110049

First published in paperback in Talking Cub
by Speaking Tiger Books in 2021

ISBN: 978-93-5447-093-6
eISBN: 978-93-5447-094-3

10 9 8 7 6 5 4 3 2 1

Printed at: Printworks, New Delhi

What Do You Want to Be When You Grow Up?

Written by
Jerry Pinto

Illustrated by
Ashok Rajagopalan

talking CUB
An Imprint of Speaking Tiger Books

I'll drive a taxi
In Cotopaxi.

I'll cure disease
With the greatest of ease.

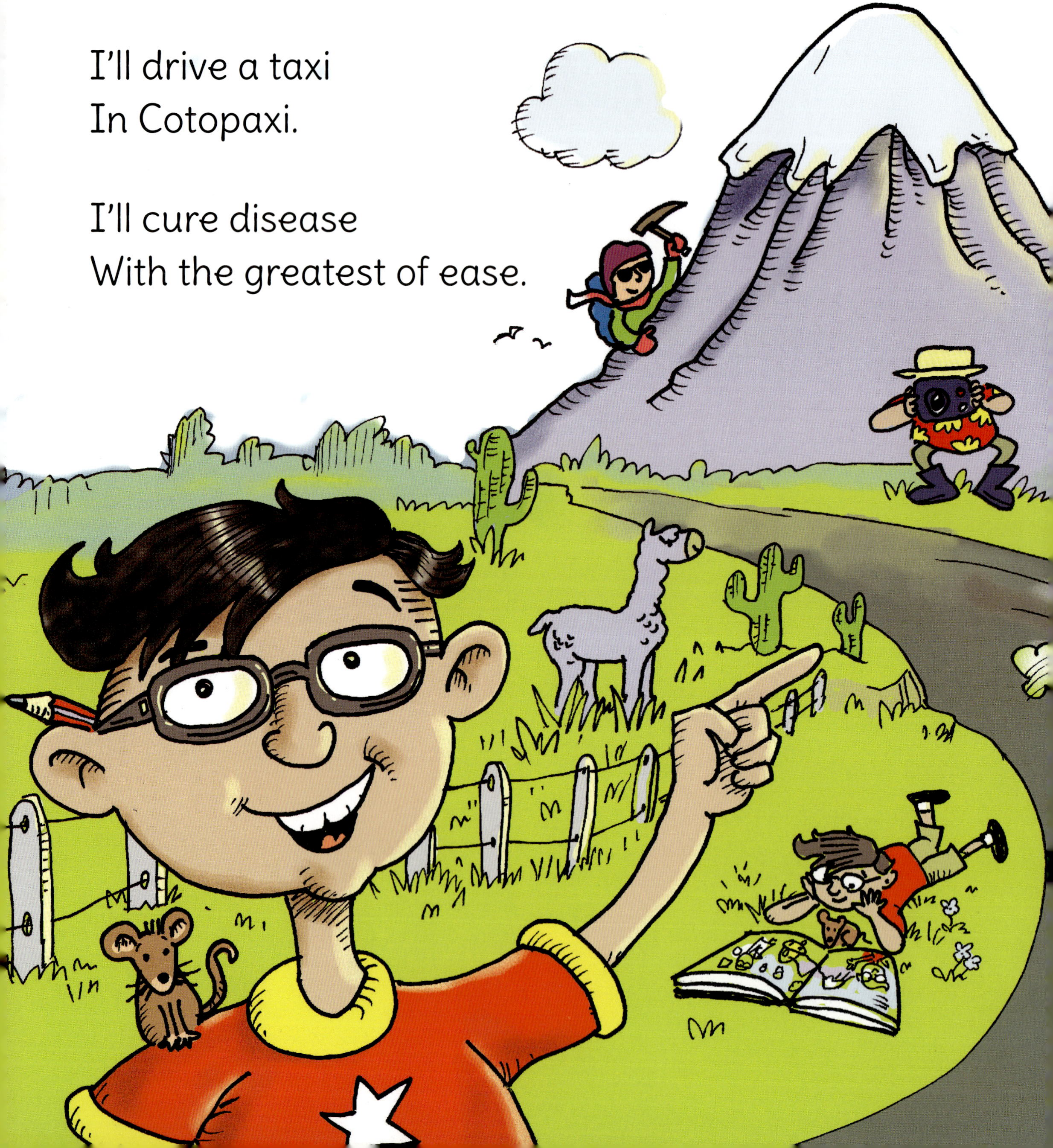

COTO
TAXi
Dr.

I'll dance with joy
At the Russian Bolshoi.

I'll win a Grammy,
And say, 'That's for Mammy.'

I'll have close shaves,
When I explore caves.

I'll go to live with Chandu Mama
And become a cabbage farmer.

I'll study with Eklavya Chacha
And become an Olympic Archer.

I'll be a book-binder
Or a great organ-grinder;

I'll be a child-minder
Or a criminal-finder.

I'll be a watch-maker
Or a lone census-taker.

I'll be a cake baker
Or a verdant lawn-raker.

I don't know yet what I want to do.
But whatever I do, what's it to you?

20
30

I'll have you know I'm only ten
Who knows what I will want when

I'm twenty or thirty or even forty?
I might be nice, I might be naughty.

I might be a banker
I might drive a tanker

Lower an anchor
Or cut off a canker.

Whatever I'll be, let me tell you chappy,
I plan to be ext-urr-emely happy.

Whatever I'll be,
I will be me.

When Jerry was wee
He thought he'd be
A tree.

When Pinto grew older
He wanted to be
A boulder.

When Jerry got brighter
He decided to be
A writer.

An illustrator of children's books since 1989, Ashok Rajagopalan's aim in life is to make people laugh. He lives in a quiet part of Chennai with his family and books.